THE TEENAGER'S ROADSIDE GUIDE TO LIFE

Preparing New Drivers for the Road Ahead

Catherine and Joe Harris
mother and son

GOLDENSTATE
PUBLISHING

Published by: Golden State Publishing
110 South Milton Ave.
Campbell, CA 95008-2806, USA

info@TeenagersRoadsideGuide.com
www.TeenagersRoadsideGuide.com

The Teenager's Roadside Guide to Life
Catherine and Joe Harris

Publisher's Cataloging-in-Publication Data
Harris, Catherine.

> The teenager's roadside guide to life : preparing new drivers for the road ahead / Catherine and Joe Harris. -- 1st ed. -- Campbell, CA : Golden State Publishing, c2004.
>
> > p. ; cm.
> > ISBN: 0-9755515-5-8
>
> > 1. Parent and teenager. 2. Teenagers and adults. 3. Adolescent psychology. 4. Automobile driver education--Psychological aspects. I. Harris, Joe. II. Title.

HQ799.15 .H37 2004
305.235--dc22   0405

Book Designer: Pamela Terry, Opus 1 Design
Editor: Brookes Nohlgren
Illustrator: Steve Ferchaud
Photographer: Dennis Burry

Special thank you to Ellen Reid. You are our "BOOK ANGEL"...you gave our book *wings*.

Printed in China

10 9 8 7 6 5 4 3 2 1
First Edition

To Jack,

On the road of life, it is not where we travel, but whom we travel with that matters. You and I were destined to take this journey together.

Love, Cath

To Dad

This is for the man who never stopped believing in me. You've taught me more than I ever thought I could learn, pushed me farther than I ever thought I could go, shown me more than I ever thought existed, and loved me more than I could ever possibly know. Without you, Dad, I wouldn't be half the man I am today, and considering that I'm not an adult yet, that really means something. You've kept my head up when I was down and picked me up when I had fallen. Mom says that you're her rock, and I've come to realize that you're mine too. You don't say much, but when you do it's important, either to make us laugh or to pass on a bit of your wisdom. I don't know what I'd do without you, or if I even could for that matter. So…this is for the man who never stopped believing in me. Thanks, Dad.

Table of Contents

Fasten Your Seat Belt!

You're in for the ride of your life.

Go confidently in the direction of your dreams,
live the life you have imagined.

–Henry David Thoreau

The road you choose is up to you.

Friends will try to persuade you. Well-meaning adults will give their advice. Family members will try to influence your decisions. But this is your life.

Where do you really want to go?

How are you going to get there?

Decide on the destination and route that are right for you. They will ultimately turn you into the person you want to become.

The greatest good you can do for another

is not just to share your riches,

but to reveal to him his own.

–Benjamin Disraeli

Your parents can't pave the road for you, but they can provide a road map.

Moms and dads can be a valuable resource. They have lots of life experience because most have been around for a long, long time.

Alone we can do so little,
together we can do so much.

–Helen Keller

Learn to merge.

Cooperation and sharing go a long way,
so don't hog the road. Life is a mutual thing.

A Lesson From Mother Nature

In Northern California we often see flocks of geese flying overhead in a V formation. We've always wondered why they fly that way, so one day we looked it up. Scientists say that by flying in formation, the whole flock can fly 71% farther than if each bird flew alone. When a goose flaps its wings it creates an updraft for the goose that follows.

As the lead goose gets tired, he will rotate to the back of the V and allow another goose to take the lead position. The geese in the back honk to encourage those in the front.

Whenever a goose falls out of formation, it immediately feels the resistance of trying to fly alone, and quickly gets back into formation.

When one of these geese gets sick or wounded and falls out of formation, two geese will follow down to help and protect it.

By sharing in each other's draft, taking turns in the lead position, honking encouragement to each other, staying in formation, and watching out for one another, the flock can accomplish so much more than if each bird flew solo. Guess we can all take a lesson from Mother Nature.

Whether you believe you can do a thing or not,

you are right.

–Henry Ford

Speed Limits

Some limits are meant to be followed,

like how fast you can go on the freeway.

Others are meant to be overcome.

The Little Engine That Could

"I think I can. I think I can." Remember the little engine that could? My mom read that book to me over and over again until I was old enough to read it myself.

Little by little parents encourage their children to do more for themselves. If kids start with "I can't" or "I don't know how" they are stopped in their tracks. Saying "I think I can" gets their engine started.

What you do speaks so loud

that I cannot hear what you say.

–Ralph Waldo Emerson

Always watch out for children.

You have a new responsibility to protect them—whether they're in your car or darting out in front of it. Either way they're going to be looking up to you. What kind of example are you setting?

Take only pictures—leave only footprints.

–Anonymous

Don't litter.

It doesn't take much effort to pick up after yourself.

Leave the path cleaner for the next person to enjoy.

What we see depends mainly on what we look for.

–John Lubbock

Blind Spots

Try to see other people and situations through God's eyes. After all, your vision is limited, but He knows exactly what is going on.

By three methods we may learn wisdom:

First, by reflection, which is noblest;

Second, by imitation, which is easiest; and

Third by experience, which is the bitterest.

–Confucius

Speed bumps are there for a reason.

Somebody didn't just put an inconvenient lump in the middle of the street for fun. It has a purpose, just like everything else does. It's there to make you THINK before you DO.

First learn the meaning of what you say, and then speak.

–Epictetus

Signals

Send yours clearly.

Read others' carefully.

The shortest distance to understanding one another

is clear communication in all that you say and do.

Character is the sum total of all the little decisions to the choices that confront us. It is a distant goal to which there is no shortcut.

–Sydney Greenberg

There are no shortcuts.

It takes time and effort to get where you want to go. If you want to be a great athlete, you need to train. If you want to be a great student, you need to study. If you want to be successful, you need to try.

Special Olympics

"Let me win, but if I cannot win, let me be brave in the attempt."

During the fall of my sophomore year in high school, my mom and I had the opportunity to work with Special Olympics, where we each coached a bowling team. A few of the participants were pretty good bowlers, others had difficulty keeping the ball in their own lane, and one occasionally rolled the ball so softly that the ball rolled back to us instead of towards the pins. One was a hugger, had to hug before and after every turn, and one never wanted to be touched. One didn't speak English, and one didn't speak at all. Each had his or her own unique and special qualities that we came to know and understand. But they all had one thing in common: they all loved bowling. They were enthusiastic and thrilled just to be there. It didn't matter if they rolled a gutter ball or a strike, they tried and tried again with their teammates, my mom, and me cheering them on. These are undoubtedly some of the most successful people we've ever known.

A person without a sense of humor

is like a wagon without springs,

jolted by every pebble in the road.

–Henry Ward Beecher

Laughter

Life's shock absorbers.

Follow your own star.

–Dante

Not every road was meant to be taken.

Listen to the voice within. Develop and refine *your* God-given talents. They will lead you on your own special journey. You don't need to take anyone else's.

When a man has not a good reason for doing a thing,
he has one good reason for letting it alone.

–Sir Walter Scott

Do not enter.

There are some places you just know you shouldn't go....So don't.

It takes time to develop character, but only a moment to get a reputation.

I will study and prepare myself
and someday my chance will come.

–Abraham Lincoln

Plan ahead.

It wasn't raining when Noah built the ark.

Happiness is not a station you arrive at,

but a manner of traveling.

–Margaret B. Runbeck

Life is not a test-drive.

You only go around the block once,

so make every mile count.

If you wish to travel far and fast, travel light.
Take off all your envies, jealousies,
unforgiveness, selfishness, and fears.

–Glenn Clark

Two-Ton Limit

Don't let the day's troubles weigh you down. You'll get a lot farther in life if you focus on the blessings.

Turn your stumbling blocks into stepping stones.

–Anonymous

Roadblocks

Adversity doesn't build character, it reveals it.

He who knows all the answers

has not yet been asked all the questions.

–Anonymous

Ask for directions.

Preferably from someone who's been where you're going. It could save you time and frustration.

Flies on the Windowsill

On my way home from running errands one day, I decided to stop at the local coffee house for a cappuccino. I took a seat in the corner facing the window. (It's my adult time-out.) There were the usual sounds of people chatting and laptops humming, but it was the buzzing that caught my attention—two little flies in a futile attempt to get out of the coffee house. The first fly sat on the windowsill and watched as the second one flew in circles. Across the room the door was open. The first fly noticed this and made *her* escape outside. Back by the window, the little insect was still flying in circles. He was lost. He didn't see the open door just a few feet away. Why didn't *he* simply ask for directions?

A real friend helps us think our best thoughts,
do our noblest deeds, be our finest selves.

–Anonymous

Choose your passengers wisely.

They can have a powerful influence on your direction. Spend your time with those who find your path agreeable and your beliefs acceptable. Steer clear of those trying to alter your course.

Live a balance life—learn some and think some and draw and paint and sing and dance and play and work every day some.

–Robert Fulghum

You won't get very far on empty.

Take time to refuel. Even the Energizer Bunny®
needs to change batteries once in a while. Nobody
can keep going…and going…and going…and
going…and going.…

Cookies and Milk Are Good for You

Whether it's energy for your body or food for your soul, we all need recharging once in a while. When Joe was just a baby cutting his first teeth, I bought teething biscuits (those hard cookies that got all over his face). It had all started when, one day, my grandmother brought over some beautiful biscotti and gave him one. *Biscotti* is the Italian word for cookies. Biscotti to help ease the pain of a new tooth, biscotti to help forget about the skinned knees after falling off his bike, biscotti after school to share the events of the day. As Joe got older, conversation was not always as forthcoming as when he was in grade school, but it didn't matter. Just sitting there, sometimes in silence, almost prayerful, was revitalizing. By the time the last swallow of milk was gone and only cookie crumbs remained, all was right with the world.

There is more to life than increasing its speed.

–Mohandas K. Gandhi

Sometimes you need to slow down.

Appreciate the wonder of every day. It's the perfect
way to allow your mind to stay open to new things.
When did you last take the time to watch the sunset?

Momma always said life was like a box of chocolates.

You never know what you're gonna get.

–Forrest Gump

It's smart to plan an alternate route.
It's wise to know when to take it.

Road conditions are often subject to weather, causing us to change course. Life conditions are just as unpredictable, so it's good to have a Plan B …just in case.

Opportunity is missed by most people
because it is dressed in overalls and looks like work.

–Thomas A. Edison

There are opportunities at every turn.

Sometimes we see them.

Sometimes we don't.

They are easier to find once we open our eyes.

A Diamond in the Rough

Every year since I was eight years old, my mom and I have gone someplace special for Mother's Day, just the two of us. Now that I'm older, I realize that this is the most generous, selfless, and loving gift my dad has given me—the gift of time to spend with my mom.

One of these trips took us to Belgium and the Netherlands. When we were in Antwerp, Belgium, we visited a diamond factory. The manager showed us an ordinary looking rock and said it was a very valuable diamond. We didn't recognize it at first because it didn't look like a diamond. The rock needed first to be cut, shaped, and polished to bring out its natural beauty.

Opportunities are like that. They are sometimes disguised as challenges and hard work. You must use your talents, abilities, and experience to polish and shape them. If you fail to look for opportunity, you will fail to see it at all. Use your special gifts so that you too may shine.

The way of progress is neither swift nor easy.

–Marie Curie

Road curves ahead.

Success rarely happens in a straight line.

Besides, it is the twists and turns

that make life interesting.

Putting off an easy thing makes it hard.

Putting off a hard thing makes it impossible.

—George Claude Lorimer

Waiting until the last minute
to make a decision and
being spontaneous are not the same.

Procrastinating will either decrease your options

or eliminate them all together.

It's better to be proactive than reactive.

Even if you're on the right track,

you'll get run over if you just sit there.

—Will Rogers

Don't idle.

When you shift into neutral, the car is neither going
nor off. Instead, it is just idling…going nowhere.
Don't let life pass you by.
Go somewhere.

To Do List:

Mow Lawn

Wash Car

Finish Homework

Go to Football Practice

Walk Dog

Clean Birdcage

Sweep Patio

Clean Room

Be thankful you have things to do today. Do them well; you will learn to have pride in all that you do. When you do your best every day, it will become a habit. This will develop your character, diligence, and a hundred other virtues that the teen who sleeps in will never know!

Now get up!

All truths are easy to understand

once they are discovered;

the point is to discover them.

–Galileo Galilei

If you want to discover new roads, you have to leave the driveway.

Growth necessitates giving up what we are familiar with for something yet unknown to us. You need to try to do something beyond what you have already mastered in order to grow mentally, spiritually, and physically.

Change your thoughts and you change your world.

–Norman Vincent Peale

When your engine sputters and stalls... consider putting in different fuel.

Think different thoughts, listen to different music, read different books. Diversity will put you far ahead of the competition because everyone else will still be caught up with yesterday's news.

We make a living by what we get.

We make a life by what we give.

–Winston Churchill

We should all plant a few trees
we may never sit under.

Do for others without expecting anything in return.

It's not *always* about you.

Let no one ever come to you without leaving better and happier. Be the living expression of God's kindness. Kindness in your face, kindness in your eyes, kindness in your smile.

–Mother Teresa

Ped X-ing

Be mindful of other people crossing your path. You
never know what kind of an impact you may have
on their lives.

The hilltop hour would not be half so wonderful

if there were no dark valleys to traverse.

–Helen Keller

You will get lost from time to time.

When you are in the dark, remember there is a light at the end of the tunnel, even if you can't see it.

Hold yourself responsible for a higher standard
than anyone else expects of you. Never excuse yourself.

–Henry Ward Beecher

Never sit in the driver's seat when you are upset.

There are hundreds of reasons for road rage,

but not one excuse.

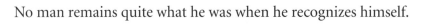

No man remains quite what he was when he recognizes himself.

–Thomas Mann

Look in the rearview mirror.

You'll see a reflection of your character.

The life which is unexamined is not worth living.

–Plato

STOP!

In the long and wonderful journey of growing, there are stops along the way. It is important to know when to stop and reflect on what you've done and where you're going.

A man who has committed a mistake

and doesn't correct it

is committing another mistake.

–Confucius

It's OK to make a U-turn.

Admitting to a mistake and correcting it
is better than continuing further off course.

I'm not there yet but I'm closer than I was yesterday.

−Anonymous

Never lose sight of the horizon.

Is what you're doing today

getting you closer

to where you want to go?

W.I.N.—What's Important Now?

Go ahead and dream big. The bigger the dream, the greater the goal you get to work for; that's what my parents have always taught me. But the way to make these dreams come true is to work towards them through the choices you make every day. That's why you need to constantly ask yourself, "What's important now?"

It doesn't matter if you want to graduate from Harvard or be an All-American. Constantly ask yourself, at least twenty-five times each day, "What's important now?"

When you first wake up, "What's important now?" Get out of bed. You need to start the day and work towards your goal.

Once you're out of bed, ask yourself again, "What's important now?" Eat a good breakfast. They don't call it the most important meal of the day for nothing. You need all the strength you can get.

"What's important now?" Go to school, study hard.

"What's important now?" Go to practice, train hard.

"What's important now?" Do whatever you need to do to get closer to your dream. Practice, study, eat right, whatever. You shouldn't be motivated to work for your goal simply because someone's watching you. You need to do it because you know it will make you better.

When you're hanging out with your friends and there are opportunities for sex, or drugs, or alcohol, guess what you should do. That's right, ask it again. "What's important now?" No matter what you're trying to be successful at, "what's important now" is to avoid these situations, because they're just going to hinder your progress and success.

A hero is no braver than an ordinary man,
but he is brave five minutes longer.

—Ralph Waldo Emerson

**Go the extra mile.
There is little traffic there.**

The distance between good and great

is not as far as you think,

so take that extra step.

Let us go singing as far as we go; the road will be less tedious.

–Virgil

Sing with the windows rolled down.

Sing like no one is watching.

The Hug

We've all been there. We're driving along, listening to a really great song, and singing our hearts out. We come to a stoplight, glance over to the car next to us, and stop singing. What's that about? We stop doing something we enjoy because someone's watching. Here's a story that reminds us not to let others make us feel self-conscious.

We were at my mother's house. She had friends visiting from out of town. My husband and son were going to go home early. They said their goodbyes and went out the door. "Wait a minute, don't I get a hug goodbye?" I asked. "Oh, Mom, I'm too big to hug anymore." (He was only seven.) I was crushed. Our friend Tony was sitting at the kitchen table. He waved his hand for Joe to come over. Now, Tony is a very, very big man. He leaned over from his chair, a few inches from Joe's face, looked him directly in the eye and said s-l-o-w-l-y, "Son, you are never, ever too big to hug your mom. She won't always be here, ya know." Joe just stood there for a moment. I didn't know if he was going to say something like "Yeah, right" or run off crying. Then he ran over to me, gave me a hug, and said, "Mom, I love you."

The next day we got to school at the same time his friend Steven did. We had our usual hug goodbye, when Steven's dad looked over at us and asked, "Aren't you too big to be hugging your mom?" I was dumbfounded. I was just about to give him a piece of my mind when I heard my son say, "No, sir. You're never too big to hug your mom."

Thank you, Tony.

The Kiss

And what about the kiss? Definitely not on the lips like when they were really young. But surely it's OK to kiss them on the cheek, right? It was in the school parking lot when he was in third grade that I kissed him goodbye and watched him walk through the playground to the spot under the flagpole where grades one through eight assembled each morning. With his back towards me I could see his right hand go up to his cheek to wipe off my kiss. He must have realized I was watching because he turned back to look at me, smiled, and said, "Just rubbing it in, Mom, so it'll last all day."

Only those who dare to fail greatly can ever achieve greatly.

–Robert Francis Kennedy

You will learn to make the right decisions only by having the freedom to make the wrong ones.

It's been said that those who do not learn from history are doomed to repeat it. When we learn from our mistakes, there are no failures, only lessons.

There are two ways of meeting difficulties:
you alter the difficulties, or you alter yourself to meet them.

–Phyllis Bottome

Emergency Kit

Patience, Understanding, Forgiveness,

Sense of Humor.

God could not be everywhere

and therefore he made mothers.

−Jewish Proverb

Call your mother when you get there.

Moms worry. That's a given. Call when you need to talk with her, and especially when you think you don't. You're never too old to let her know that you're OK, and to say, "I love you."

Do what you can, with what you have, where you are.

–Theodore Roosevelt

Accelerate your life.

Now that you're in the driver's seat, are you willing to venture out onto roads that you've never seen before? Or are you just going to follow the same beaten path that everyone else has taken? Don't worry about failing, everyone fails at something. Worry about not trying. Have faith and believe in yourself. You will always find your way home.

A smile is the lighting system of the face,

the cooling system of the head, and

the heating system of the heart.

—Anonymous

It's not about the car.
(well...sort of)

Life isn't about what you're driving. Life is about
what's driving you...to succeed, to serve others, to
grow spiritually, to be the best you can be. Life is a
journey. But at the end of your journey, whichever
path you choose, God won't care what kind of car
you drove, but only what kind of driver you were.

From Infant Car Seat to Driver's Seat

Baby Steps

Remember when our children first learned to walk? They stood up kind of wobbly on their little legs. We stood a few steps away, our arms stretched out towards them, "Come on, you can do it, come to Mommy," we encouraged. They started slowly and then took rapid little steps as they fell into our arms, grinning from ear to ear. "Yeah! You did it!" we praised. We backed up farther so they could do it again. They became more confident with each and every step they took, and their world changed forever. With their newfound mobility came curiosity, and every day was an adventure.

We can all recall the morning the cabinets with the pots and pans were discovered. It was a source of entertainment for hours or until we could no longer stand the "music." In those days we kept our little ones safe by baby-proofing their world. We installed locks on cabinets containing cleaning supplies. We bought those little plastic plugs for electrical outlets. Breakables were packed and put away. We padded coffee tables and everything else that had sharp corners. We were our children's protectors. They trusted us to keep them safe, and we did. That was a time when most boo-boos could be healed with Band-Aids®, kisses, and hugs.

Vrroom Vrroom

Before you know it, they are walking all over the house, leaving toys everywhere. One of my son's favorite toys was an oversized plastic car with small pudgy people. He placed the boy in the driver's seat and arranged his passengers in the back. "Vrroom, Vrroom." He'd make that engine sound, and then off he went on his imaginary journey. As he got bigger, his cars and trucks got smaller. I once found fabric that had colorful roadways on it and glued it to cardboard, creating an instant city. "Vrroom, Vrroom." I could hear the sounds of a boy happily playing with cars in his room, where he was safe. He had lots of little vehicles, including a fire truck and an ambulance with a siren. I never liked the sound of the siren.

First Road Trip

We had just returned from a trip to the market. My son helped me carry in the groceries. He had become such a big boy. As I was putting things away I could see him make several trips from his room back out to the car, each time carrying out another toy. A few minutes later, he asked if he could make lunch. He got out the bread, climbed up on the footstool, and made four peanut butter and jelly sandwiches. "You must be really hungry." "Mom, they're not all for me, they're for our trip." "What trip?" "Me and the guys. We're going to the park and I'm driving." I followed him outside to the car. There was JJ, his stuffed dog, in the front seat. Michelangelo, Leonardo, Donatelo, and Rafael—his Ninja Turtles—were in the back. He climbed into the driver's seat and grabbed the steering wheel. I adjusted the seat as far forward as it could go. He couldn't even see over the dash, and his feet didn't reach the pedals, but he didn't seem to mind. He had a big grin on his face as he waved goodbye and said, "Don't worry, Mom, I'll be OK." I went back into the house and watched through the window. He sat in the car in the driveway, and he was safe. If they could just stay little a little longer....

He Used a Whole Tank of Gas
and Never Left the Driveway

He is still in the driveway. This time the seat is adjusted as far back as it can go. At 6'1" he needs all the legroom he can get. The radio is so loud the car is vibrating, even before he turns on the ignition. Vrroom, vrroom. There is that familiar sound again. Only this time it's real. I see the car back out of the driveway, and then race forward. I hear the brakes squeal. With only his permit, he can't be on the road without a licensed driver, and he wants to drive every chance he gets, even if it's only in the driveway. Back and forth, back and forth. "Time to come in," I yell out the window. Of course he doesn't hear me over the music. I go out to the car and in my loudest voice, "DINNER IS READY!" just as the song ends. "Gee, Mom, you don't have to yell."

It's Like a Ride at Disneyland

If you enjoy amusement park rides, you will love teaching your teenager to drive a stick shift. I'm not talking about the little teacups or the merry-go-round types, but more like the kind that toss you from side to side in a jerking motion. The ones with the health warning before you climb in. You know, do not go on this ride if: you suffer from back pain, have a heart condition, have high blood pressure, or get frightened easily.

It is best to practice in a wide-open area, free of other moving vehicles—free of any vehicles for that matter. A church parking lot when there were no services scheduled was our choice. My son and I switched seats, and I explained about the clutch and the RPMs and how the gears are arranged in the figure H. "I know, Mom," he said impatiently. "It shows it right here on the gearshift knob." "Let's just start out slowly. When you want to change gears, push in the clutch when you shift." I barely finished my sentence when he stepped on the accelerator, revved the engine to a million RPMs and popped the clutch. The car lurched forward, bounced, and stalled. "OK, this is going well, let's try it again. Just give it a little less gas and easy on the clutch." I braced myself. He turned on the ignition, stepped on the clutch, and floored it. If he had popped the clutch then I wouldn't have to worry about him hitting that parked car because we would surely have catapulted right over it. "What are you doing, trying to get us killed?" "You said give it a LITTLE less gas." "Let's just try it again." After many take-offs and landings, we decided to call it quits for the day. "I think you did a good job." I tried to sound encouraging. "You are very talented. I have never known anyone who can stop the car twenty-seven times without ever touching the brakes. So what did you think of your first lesson?" I asked. "I think Dad should teach me, no offense." "None taken."

A Teen's Dream, a Parent's Nightmare

Today is a dream for teens, a nightmare for parents—the day of the driver's test. They have had their driving permit for six months, can back the car out of the driveway and listen to music at the same time. They are capable of changing lanes, but still drive too fast. They practice every chance they get and we have the grey hairs to prove it. Every time they get in the driver's seat, they have a huge grin on their face, just like when they were learning to walk. The only difference is now if we stood out in front to encourage them, we just might get run over.

They are sixteen and this is no baby step, this is huge. It is so much more than driving the car. It is about freedom. Freedom to go where they want, when they want, without their parents. It is a rite of passage to becoming an adult. Their world just got bigger.

In few other countries is driving a car so important. That's it. Maybe, we should move to China where bicycles are the mode of transportation. There are many parts of the world where mothers send their sons off on llamas or camels, but they have other worries I'm sure. A tiny part of me hopes he won't pass, and I can keep him safe just a little longer.

Got Milk?

If you've got a new driver in the house, chances are you've "got milk," and bread, and cereal, and whatever other items you might need on a moment's notice.

Never before has your teenager been so eager to run errands for you. Need a prescription filled? Not a problem. The clothes at the cleaners need to be picked up? Consider it done. They have car keys in hand and are out the door in a flash. And the sibling they couldn't stand to be near before they got their driver's license is now their new best friend. They will cheerfully chauffeur them to and from school, soccer practice, and just about anywhere, if it means they can drive the car.

God Called "Shotgun"

It's not that we think our sons and daughters are bad drivers, because after all, we taught them. It is just that overcrowded freeways, rush-hour traffic, and rude, reckless, road-raged motorists are undesirable for any driver. Now add the inexperienced teen, and the fact that most think that they are invincible. That is a scary thought indeed.

I have never prayed so much as I do when my son gets behind the wheel of a car. I cannot be with him all the time now (nor does he want me to be), so I'm letting God ride in the passenger seat.

A Key of Their Own

Handing over the car keys with all of its implications is not an easy thing to do. Ahead of our children stretches their future like a road leading into the distance. Along that road they will need to make choices.

The Roadside Guide is meant to be a source of inspiration to prepare teens for the real world and to help them learn to make smart decisions.

Whether you read the whole book in one sitting or one sign at a time, you will be amazed at the wonderful conversations you and your sons and daughters will have. You will be reminded of just how much they've grown and matured. You will come to realize that they really are ready to sit in the driver's seat, and that we need to move over.

What's Your Story?

Everybody has one. Would you like to share yours? Tell us about your experience of getting your driver's license. Does it illustrate one of the principles in this book? If you would like to share your story and submit it for possible inclusion in a future book, please go to *www.TeenagersRoadsideGuide.com* and tell us about it. Or send it to:

Golden State Publishing
110 South Milton Ave.
Campbell, CA 95008-2806
USA